all wired up

MARK LAREAU

A BEADWORK
HOW-TO BOOK

 INTERWEAVE PRESS

Editor, Judith Durant
Technical editor, Dorothy T. Ratigan
Illustration, Gayle Ford
Photography, except as noted, Joe Coca
Design and production, Dean Howes
Cover design, Bren Frisch
Copy editor, Stephen Beal

Beadwork Magazine

Interweave Press
201 East Fourth Street
Loveland, Colorado 80537-5655 USA
www.interweave.com

Printed in the United States by Kendall Printing Company

Library of Congress Cataloging-in-Publication Data

Lareau, Mark,
   All wired up : wire techniques for the beadworker and jewelry maker : a beadwork
how-to book / Mark Lareau.
      p. cm.
   Includes index.
   ISBN 1-883010-73-X
   1. Wire craft. 2. Jewelry making. 3. Beadwork. I. Title.

TT214.2 .L37 2000
745.58'2—dc21   00-040764

First printing: IWP—10M:700:KP
Second printing: IWP—5M:401:KP
Third printing: IWP—6M:1101:KP

Acknowledgements

First and foremost I would like to thank Viki, without whose unwavering love, support, and strength I would be nobody. It is without question her unapologetic promotion and marketing of and faith in me through the years that have made this book possible.

While not really a "thank you," I would like to acknowledge my three wonderful children, Trevor, Julian, and Sophia, and the fact that this book would have been produced much sooner if I hadn't had so many damn pancakes to flip.

I would like to thank Judith Durant (a.k.a. "Uber-Editor"), whose gentle tutelage and kind prodding turned my happy little manuscript into this awesome book, which far exceeded my expectations. I can't thank you as I should.

I would like to thank my brother Ed, for your moral(e) support all these years I've lived so far away from where I was born. There is perhaps no truer indication in my mind of the wacky nature of the universe when someone who is "making it up as they go" (like me) gets to write a book before someone who is truly talented (like my brother Ed).

I would also like to thank my sister Louise, my Mom, and my Dad.

I owe a lot to all the wonderful wire artists I've ever met (especially the ones I borrowed technique from!), and all the wonderful students I've ever had (the ones I tried out the techniques I borrowed from all the great wire artists on), and all the wonderful staff we've ever had at The Bead Factory for their support.

Table of Contents

Introduct[ion]

My main reason for writ[ing...]
the huge need for it. M[...]
books available at th[...]
ing are either far too complex [...]
wireworker, or woefully inad[...]
descriptions of the techniqu[...]
cessful wireworking. In ad[...]
available books focus on [...]
bly-difficult-to-construct [...]
made with square wire [...]
wireworker, round wi[...]
able and economical[...]
introduce the begin[...]
and, I hope, aid th[...]
progressively diffi[...]

Wire Finishes

Plated wire is just that—wire of a base metal, usually aluminum, copper, or nickel, that has been plated with a coating to give it a color or the look of a solid precious metal such as gold or silver. There are some astonishing col-

Wire

Wire for beadwork and jewelry making comes in a wide array of styles, materials, finishes, hardnesses, and sizes.

Wire Styles and Materials

Available styles include round, half-round, square, and triangular wire. The terms are literal, describing what the wire looks like when viewed in profile. The wirework presented throughout this book is done with round wire and I recommend using good quality sterling-plated or sterling-filled wire. Sterling, gold, gold-filled, copper, or even brass will also work, but it may be difficult to find these wires in the half-hard variety (I'll explain this below). Good wire may be available from your local bead store, or you may mail-order wire. (See page 126 for a list of resources.) Whatever you do, don't go to the hardware store and buy spools of the soft copper alloy wire available there; it is just too soft to work effectively.

ored wires available, but the color coating is either nylon or baked-on enamel that easily scratches off, so I don't recommend them for pieces that will be worn or frequently handled.

When it comes to precious-metal wires, the term gold-filled (or rolled gold) sometimes causes confusion, even within the jewelry industry. The term usually precedes a number ratio, such as "gold-filled" 14/20. This means that 14 karat gold 1/20th the weight of the overall product is heat- and pressure-bonded to the outside of a core of another metal, usually copper or sterling silver. Hence gold-filled actually means a coating of gold that contains a filling (sort of like a Twinkie, only not as resistant to the ravages of time). And don't be too quick to dismiss gold-filled wire as some plated upstart—the 1/20th layer on the core is actually much thicker than a standard micron-thin plate. The interior core can never leach out onto the surface, so even if you're allergic to copper you can safely wear a gold-filled earring that has a copper core.

Wire Hardnesses

Hardness is another variable quality of wire. I heartily recommend using wire that is half-hard. Half-hard wire has been treated in one of two ways. Either it has been annealed or it has been drawn through a tiny hole in a steel plate to a size smaller than it originally was. Annealed wire has been heated to around 600°F (315°C) and then slowly cooled. This process strengthens the wire and prevents brittleness. Drawing makes the wire thinner, but it also realigns the crystalline structure of the metal, making it stiffer (which is good), but at the same time more brittle (which is bad).

Much of the excellent German plated and filled wire that is now available is half-hard, but you'll have to ask your merchant to be absolutely sure. A lot of the wire sold today is "dead-soft," which is to say that no extra processing (annealing or drawing) has been done after fabrication. Dead-soft wire offers no resistance when you're working with it. This quality may initially seem to be an asset, but it actually makes the wire very difficult to work with.

If you grasp a piece of dead-soft wire with flat nose pliers and try to make a sharp right angle bend, the wire turns limply to make a weak and curving bend. Half-hard wire is ideal for wirework because the wire resists you every step of the way. It doesn't want to bend, less of its surface yields, thus it makes a sharp angle.

Wire Sizes

In North America, the most readily available wire sizes range from 26-gauge to 14-gauge. These numbers are somewhat arbitrary, but in general the smaller the number, the thicker the wire. Just about everywhere else in the world, wire is measured by its actual diameter in

Wire Sizes

Gauge Size	Approximate Diameter (in Millimeters)
26	0.4mm
24	0.5mm
22	0.6mm
20	0.8mm
18	1.0mm
16	1.3mm
14	1.6 mm

millimeters. The chart shown above gives you an idea of what size the gauges are, and vice-versa. Most projects and techniques presented in this book are done with 20-gauge (0.8mm) wire. I like this size because, when the wire is half-hard, it is stiff enough to hold its shape nicely, but not so stiff that you have to possess Herculean strength to work with it. It is just the right size for ear wires and headpins, looks great in a wirewrap, and is never so big that it overwhelms the piece it is holding together. A few projects call for 18-gauge (1.0mm) wire. Just because no project in this book incorporates other sizes of wire doesn't mean they aren't useful in certain situations. Some semiprecious stones will shatter if skewered onto a 20-gauge wire, while some free-form elements or huge clasps may fall into a useless pile of scrap metal unless they're made with wire much bigger than 18-gauge.

Tools

Good-quality pliers are essential for your enjoyment of wireworking as well as for professional-looking results. Before you buy pliers, look at them from every angle, paying particular attention to the shape of the nose. This is important because each kind of pliers does only one thing—pull the wire onto the shape of its nose. Round nose pliers have circular tips, chain nose pliers have half-circular tips, flat nose pliers have rectangular tips.

As a general rule, I recommend that you buy the most expensive pair of pliers you can afford. There are some very high-quality Swedish pliers out there, but in my opinion they are overpriced (so much for rules!). German-made pliers tend to be better value for your dollar than most, although the quality of some Pakistani-made pliers (the chain nose and flat nose type in particular) has increased dramatically in recent years. The problem with Pakistani round nose pliers is that the noses are very rarely truly round, but rather oval, and it's really hard to make perfect circular loops with an oval pair of pliers! If possible, buy at least one good pair of German-made round nose pliers, and a really good pair of flush cutters.

The Essentials

Here's a short list of tools you'll need to complete any of the projects in this book.

Round Nose Pliers are far and away the most important tool a wireworker owns. You cannot properly make loops with any other pair of pliers. I like German-made rosary pliers. The round nose offers a great variance of size, from the tiny points all the way up to the huge box (or trunk) of the pliers. The great thing about these big heavy-duty pliers is that you can work them hard and they seem to last forever. You would go through many pairs of lesser-quality pliers during the life span of this one, so all in all they're a great value. Unfortunately, the cutting edge on these pliers is plagued with the same problem most cutters have: They don't make a nice flush cut.

Flush Cutters are the next most important pair of pliers you will own. Make sure that they will cut wire absolutely flush, leaving a little wedge-shaped burr only on one end. Before you buy a pair of cutters, cut a piece of wire with them. Look at both cut ends. Very likely one will have the wedge-shaped burr. If the other end doesn't, but rather is nice and flat, then you have my permission to buy the pliers. Try to find a pair that comes to a nice point so you can get into tight spaces and cut small pieces off the ends of wire wraps.

Chain Nose Pliers are so-called because you use them to open and close small chain links. They are very often (mistakenly) referred to as needle nose pliers, which are electrical tools. The major difference between chain nose pliers and needle nose pliers is that the chain nose has no teeth to mar your wirework. Chain nose pliers are extremely useful in many situations, especially for opening and closing small loops, getting into tight spaces, and crimping down the ends of wire wraps. They're far and away my favorite—if you have to make a choice between chain nose and flat nose pliers (see page 12), chain nose are the way to go.

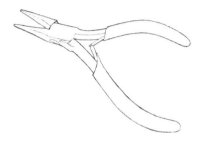

Other Useful Tools

I would say that 90 percent of my wirework is done with only the above three tools, but here are some other useful tools. We'll use all of them in the scope of this book, but most good wirework can be done without them.

Wire Straightening (or Nylon Jaw) Pliers
While not an essential tool, wire straightening pliers are really helpful if you have trouble straightening wire with your fingers. They also work like magic for smoothing out nasty little kinks. If you need justification to purchase them beyond the fact that you may not (yet) have enough finger strength to perfectly straighten wire, consider the following: Very often the ends of a spool of wire are twisted into very nasty kinks. Usually you snip those pieces off and trash them, wasting a few inches of wire and, therefore, money. If you had these pliers, you could straighten out those kinked ends and use the wire. In no time at all, my set paid for themselves many times over!

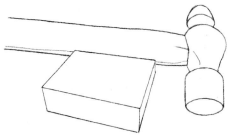

Flat Nose Pliers are very much like chain nose pliers, except that rather than tapering down, they stay nice and wide all the way to the tips. These are helpful when you want to hold onto several pieces of wire stacked one on top of the other and for making nice sharp right-angle bends.

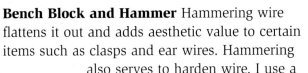

Bench Block and Hammer Hammering wire flattens it out and adds aesthetic value to certain items such as clasps and ear wires. Hammering also serves to harden wire. I use a nice, small 2½" steel bench block and a regular old 8-ounce ball-peen hammer. Some people prefer smaller hammers, but for whacking really big wire the 8-ounce ball-peen is way more fun!

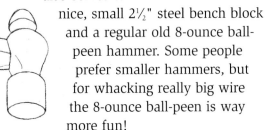

Crimp Forming Pliers These specialty pliers are made to use with crimping beads (the soft metal beads that you smash onto tigertail to finish it off and keep it from raveling). The inside station has a little tooth in one side that bends the bead into a **U**, and the outside station forms the crimped bead into a smooth round sleeve. We won't use these for crimping but for building wire cages, and we'll only use the outside (smoothing) station.

Tool Magic ® Rubber Coating This is a terrific product that I use to coat the tips of pliers with a heavy-duty rubber coating. It lets you grip your wire firmly without marring it. We will be doing a lot of flat scrolls in this book, and pliers dipped in this coating will make your life much easier while scrolling.

Needle Files or Cup Burrs We will use these to de-burr wire ends, especially when we're making ear wires. A needle file is just that—a very fine file used in metalsmithing. A cup burr is like a small drill bit you can use in a Dremel tool. The burr is shaped like a tiny cup at the end, and it has small teeth inside that smooth out the ends of wire.

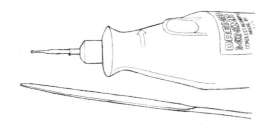

Chapter Two

GETTING STARTED

In order to fully enjoy wirework, it is essential not only that your projects be successful, but that you are comfortable and happy while working. Here are some basic strategies to get you started down the right path.

Work with Clean Hands

Perspiration and body oils can dramatically enhance the tarnishing process. If your hands tend to sweat a lot, wash them before and occasionally during a project. Also be sure to dry your hands thoroughly. Damp fingers can be quite slippery, and are almost certainly prone to soreness while working with wire. Don't use hand creams or lotions before starting a wire-work project.

Mind Your Posture

Try to work sitting in a comfortable chair with your back straight. The most common cause of fatigue, headaches, and neck tension while doing wirework is what I call the Quasimodo Syndrome. I've seen it a thousand times. People start a project with relaxed, perfect posture, but within ten or fifteen minutes the shoulders start creeping up. By the time an hour rolls around, they're all hunched over looking for cathedral bells to ring. Most people don't even realize they are hunching, so all I can do is point it out and hope you'll be conscious of your posture. Try to keep your shoulders lower than your collarbone and in a straight line with your torso.

How to Hold Your Pliers

Try to remember that you are doing wire-work with jewelry tools, not microsurgery with delicate medical instruments. Holding pliers in the tips of your fingers will never give you the amount of control you need to use the tool

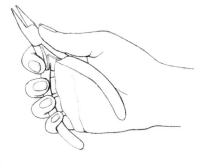

effectively. Hold pliers in the palm of your hand with one side running along the ball of your thumb, the other across all your fingers. Some people find it comfortable to place their thumb flat against the box of the pliers.

While doing research for this part of the book, I consulted two medical specialists, an occupational therapist and a neurosurgeon, about the use of pliers. Both specialists confirmed that the big problem with using pliers is repeated hyperextension of the wrist, which causes micro-tears in the tendons. These micro-tears don't cause any immediate discomfort, and they heal naturally enough. However, repeated tearing and healing causes an insidious build-up of scar tissue, which can eventually produce the dreaded carpal tunnel syndrome and other nasty ailments. So, generally, try not to angle your hand too far back while working. Anything approaching ninety degrees is a no-no.

Another gesture that can cause problems is squeezing the pliers too hard. Relax. Fulcrum dynamic principle states that the force exerted by the shorter end (the nose) of a non-equidistant dual cantilever (the pliers) is exponentially greater that the force placed at the longer end (the handles) by a factor of . . . . (It actually gets pretty technical from here on out—lots of math!) Just take my word for it: You don't need a death-grip on those pliers; a little finesse goes a long way.

Work with a Useable Length of Wire

Wire can become unwieldy in long pieces. Unless you have a certain project in mind that requires long pieces, try not to cut a working length of wire that exceeds the distance from your fingertips to the inside of your elbow.

Straightening Wire

While many artistic individuals will argue this point, people tend to be able to follow straight lines with their eyes easier than curved ones. By extension, straight lengths of wire tend to be easier to work with than curved pieces. Much of the wire sold in bead shops and jewelry supply stores is packaged in neat attractive coils. To prepare a piece of such wire for a project, I recommend you straighten it. This technique is sort of the opposite of what you do with a curling ribbon. With a little practice, you can get most types and gauges of wire to become almost perfectly straight. You may use a pair of wire straightening pliers or just your fingers. Both methods require that you develop a little finesse.

Straightening Wire with Fingers

1 Cut a length of wire and hold one end in your non-dominant hand with chain nose pliers.

2 Grasp the wire just under the pliers with the fingers of your dominant hand. (If you don't want to get your fingers dirty, use a paper towel or a clean rag.)

3 Squeezing slightly, pull the entire length of wire through your fingers. Best results are obtained when slightly more pressure is applied to the outer side of the coiled wire. Repeat a couple of times until the wire is more or less straight.

Straightening Wire with Pliers

1 Cut a length of wire and hold one end of it in your non-dominant hand with chain nose pliers.

2 Using your dominant hand, grasp the wire just under the chain nose pliers with your wire straightening pliers.

3 Squeezing slightly, pull along the entire length of wire through the wire straightening pliers. Repeat as necessary until the wire is more or less straight.

Note that the wire has to be more or less perpendicular to the jaws of the wire straightening pliers. If it isn't, you will pull your wire into another curve.

Polishing Your Wirework

Most wirework can be polished with commercially available jewelry buffing pads. If you want to use a cleaning solution, be sure to test a spare piece of wire in the solution before dropping in any finished work.

Chapter 3

BASIC WIREWORK TECHNIQUES

Before getting started on that fabulous piece of jewelry you've been dreaming about, it's important to become comfortable working with wire and to master a few basic techniques. In this chapter you'll learn how to make perfect loops and scrolls. These are the bases for many of the projects that follow.

Perfect Simple Loops

Making perfect loops is the single most important task in wirework. And yet it's the one task most often performed improperly. Why? Poor technique and use of tools not suited to the job. While these two errors cause problems in all areas of wirework, nowhere are the problems more obvious than in a simple loop.

My definition of a perfect simple loop is one that is perfectly round, closed, and centered on the wire from which it is formed.

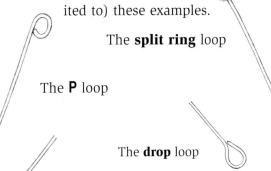

The **perfect** simple loop

Common malformations of loops include (but are by no means limited to) these examples.

The **split ring** loop

The **P** loop

The **drop** loop

The **egg** loop

The **almost-there** loop

The first few times you try making perfect loops is a lot like the first few times you sit behind the wheel of a car. There's a lot to keep in the front of your mind. "Am I speeding? Which mirror should I look into? Am I centered in the lane? What is that maniac doing? Was that a police car I just blew past? What's that flashing on my dashboard?" But after a few weeks of driving, you become very comfortable with the process and feel you could do it in your sleep. (In fact, I have often argued that many drivers where I live seem to do just that.) Making a perfect loop is very much the same exercise in growth. With a little practice, you'll get comfortable with the process, and eventually you'll be able to make loops in your sleep (which is not, however, recommended).

After years of trying every conceivable method of making loops, I've found that the technique shown here yields the most consistent results. However, if you've been making loops any other way, and they come out looking like our "perfect" example, feel free to ignore this entire section. (On second thought, you may want to try it my way.)

Grab a few beads that your wire will fit through and start as follows.

1 Using a 6" length, make a nice sharp 90° bend with the first ½" inch of the wire. Actually, the amount of wire to bend back will vary greatly depending on how big a loop you want to make. For purposes of illustration I bent back ½" of wire, but you will have to play around a bit until you figure out just how much wire you'll need to bend back for the size loop you want. At first, try making loops at the same point on the round nose pliers. This practice will enable you to see whether you are using too little or too much wire for your loop. You may actually want to mark a small guideline on your pliers to facilitate loop making.

2 Hold the wire vertically in front of you, with the bent piece pointing towards you. Hold the round nose pliers up between you and the end of the wire, with your palm facing out.

3 Grasp the very tip of the wire with the round nose pliers. Begin forming the loop by twisting the round nose pliers up and away from you. Keep the tip of the pliers in the same point in space with the 90° bend coming toward you, and be careful not to pull out the bend as you go.

4 When you've completed about half a loop (usually when your hand gets to that awkward position that causes your elbows to creep down and touch each other) *stop.*

5 Opening your pliers slightly, slide them back a half-turn. Close the pliers lightly onto the half-formed loop and continue, paying particular attention to the fact that you must keep the entire half-formed loop "filled" with your pliers. If you don't do this, but grasp the loop close to the tip of your pliers, the loop will become malformed. Continue this way, pulling a quarter turn at a time, until the loop is closed.

6 Slide a bead onto the wire so that it is right up against the loop you've just made. Push the wire over onto the bead with your fingers so that it comes out of the bead at a 90° angle.

7 Now here's where getting to know how much wire you'll need to make your loop becomes more critical. Snip the wire down to ½" (so the loop on both sides of the bead is the same size).

8 Hold the bead with the wire oriented so that it faces towards you. Grasp the tip of the wire with the round nose pliers (again making sure that you start with your palm out).
Form this loop using the same method as for the previous one, following Steps 3–5.

The practical uses for this kind of loop are endless. When you're making earrings, you can start with a headpin, string a bead on it, make a loop, and attach the loop to an ear wire. Variations on this technique are also endless. Add more beads and dangles by making loops on both sides of beads and connect them together as creativity dictates. Necklaces and bracelets are particularly impressive when linked this way (not to mention the fact that it takes far fewer beads to make a necklace this way, as opposed to stringing beads all together side by side).

Opening and Closing Loops

There is only one way to open and close the loops in the end of wire (like the ones you've just made), whether they're in the bottom of ear wires, in eyepins, or in jump rings. Grasp the "open" side of the loop with two pairs of pliers and twist slightly outwards. You'll know you've done this correctly if the loop still looks closed when viewed from the side. You can then link whatever you want onto the loop and close it up by twisting in the reverse direction. If you do this properly, you won't have to "fine tune" the loop after you have opened and closed it. You won't have altered its roundness, so it'll end the way it began.

Wrapped Loops

A wrapped loop is just like a regular loop except the wire doesn't end at the right-angle bend at the bottom of the loop, but continues on to wrap around the stem wire. While several techniques are commonly used, I like this one best for two very good reasons. First, because you are watching the entire loop being formed, it will turn out perfect every time—there's just no way to mess it up. Second, you don't have to change the position of your round nose pliers—once you've started, you don't ever have to let go of the wire until the loop is completely formed.

This method of loop making is especially useful when you're linking one or two beads as a component in an earring or pendant. And although it may be rather time-consuming to complete an entire necklace using this technique, the results can be dramatic. An "endless" necklace so made would in most cases be so sturdy that you'd more than likely break your neck before you broke your necklace. Generally I suggest you add a clasp (like one of the wire clasps discussed later in this book) to provide a safety escape from subway trains, freight elevators, or anything else you may find yourself "hung up" on.

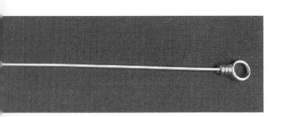

1 Using a piece of wire that is about 6½" long, bend (with chain nose pliers) the first 3" over into a nice sharp 90° angle. Try to think of this bend as "sacred." You don't ever want to lose this bend.

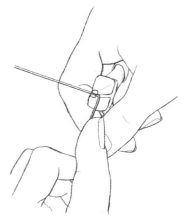

2 Now hold your round nose pliers about ¼"
away from the bend. As you do when forming a regular loop,
hold the wire pointing
towards you and your
plier-hand facing
palm outwards. Tilt
your head
sideways so that
you are more or
less looking down
the points of your
round nose pliers.
Start to loop the
wire up and over

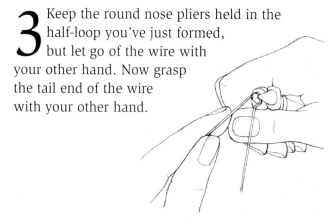

by rolling the pliers away from you. As with the
regular loops, be sure that the wire and pliers are
perpendicular to each other. You'll stop looping at
a very specific moment, which can be described
in one of two ways. First, imagine that the loop is
complete. If the imagined completed loop is "centered" over the wire, stop
bending. *Or* when you get
to the point that, if you
were to continue rolling
you'd pull out the
sacred bend you
made in Step 1,
stop bending.

3 Keep the round nose pliers held in the
half-loop you've just formed,
but let go of the wire with
your other hand. Now grasp
the tail end of the wire
with your other hand.

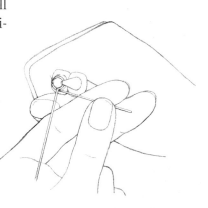

Continue to pull
the tail onto the pli-
ers, behind the
half-loop, until
the loop is com-
pletely formed and
the tail end con-
tinues out per-
pendicular to
the piece of
wire the whole
thing started
from.

4 Holding your chain nose pliers in your non-dominant hand with the nose pointing straight out in front of you, grasp the loop. The long piece of wire you'll be wrapping should be perpendicular to the pliers, and the tail end you pulled around the pliers to form the loop should be pointing straight out away from you.

Holding the loop firmly in your pliers, begin pulling the tail end around the other end. Make sure that both the piece of wire you are wrapping with and the piece of wire you are wrapping around are perpendicular to each other. This will ensure nice tight wraps.

Try to avoid "pushing" the wire onto itself with your index finger. Rather, "pull" the wire from as far away as you can hold onto it. I always put a small bend in the end of the wire I'm pulling so that I have more leverage when I'm wrapping.

5 After you've pulled three or four wraps, snip the tail of wire off with flush cutters as close as you can to the shaft of wire you've been wrapping it onto.

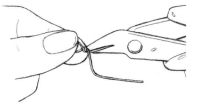

Tweak the tail down lightly onto the shaft with your chain nose pliers.

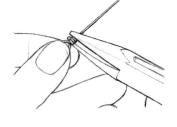

Now that you've completed one wrapped loop, let's use it in an actual jewelry design situation.

6 String a bead onto the shaft of wire that ends in the wrapped loop. Grasp the wire near the tip of your chain nose pliers right up against the bead.

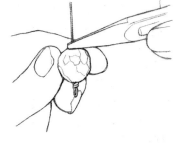

Exactly how far up the chain nose you'll grasp the wire will depend on how many wraps you have between the loop and the bead. You'll see what I mean in a minute.

Make a nice sharp 90° bend onto the top of your pliers

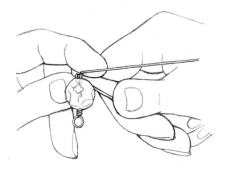

7 Make a wrapped loop as in Steps 2–4. The last wrap should end right up against the bead.

In future attempts you can adjust the number of wraps you make by changing the length of wire from the bend to the bead. To make fewer wraps, place the chain nose right up against the bead close to the tip of the pliers. To make more wraps, place the tip farther away from the bead.

8 Snip off the tail as close as you can to the bead.

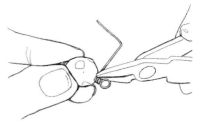

Tweak the tail down onto the shaft right up against the bead.

For argument's sake, let's say you want to make a whole necklace of wrapped loops. You have to connect one loop to the next before you wrap the next loop closed. Here's what I mean.

9 Make another wrapped loop, starting from Step 1. Stop when you get to the point where you've made the loop on the other side, but you haven't started wrapping.

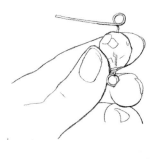

10 String the tail end of the wire of the loop you've just formed into one loop of the completed unit. Pull it all the way on until the two loops are interconnected.

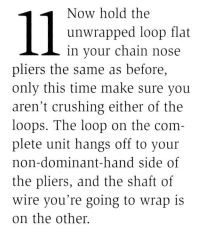

11 Now hold the unwrapped loop flat in your chain nose pliers the same as before, only this time make sure you aren't crushing either of the loops. The loop on the complete unit hangs off to your non-dominant-hand side of the pliers, and the shaft of wire you're going to wrap is on the other.

12 Now finish wrapping the shaft up to the bead as before, snip, tweak, and you're done.

You can continue this way, linking pieces together one at a time, until you've completed an entire piece. The real beauty of this technique is that if you forget to link two beads together when you're making the first wrapped loop, you can always link them up on the other side.

Scrolls

There are lots of uses for these flat scrolls. Many of the projects in this book use them, so please don't skip this section! Some people call these forms spirals, but I always think of a spiral as a swirling vortex, very three-dimensional. I really want to convey a sense of "flatness" here, so I will call them scrolls.

1 Start with a 6" piece of wire. Pull the wire straight using one of the methods shown on page 17.

2 Make the start of a tiny **P** at one end of the wire by grasping the very end of it in the tip (smallest part) of your round nose pliers. You should try to actually "smash" the wire into a small curving wedge when you do this, so the very tip of the wire is sharp enough to scroll smoothly onto itself.

3 Keep bending the **P** over so it begins to scroll sideways onto itself (you want this form to look like a cinnamon or jelly roll, not a coil or pig's tail). Stop when the round nose pliers touch the wire.

4 Now grasp the partially formed scroll flat in the chain nose. Make sure you can see where the wire comes off the beginning of the scroll.

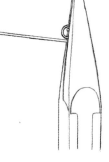

5 Now "pull" the wire up onto the scroll. You should grasp the scroll firmly enough that it won't slip in your chain nose, but not so firmly that you flatten it and mar the wire. Repeat this process, building the scroll up a quarter turn at a time.

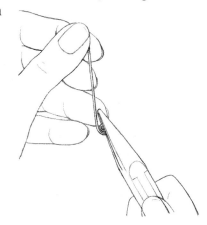

6 Once you've completed your scroll, you can slide the chain nose pliers into the small space where the wire comes off the scroll and then bend the wire up, away from it. Stop bending when the wire is at a 90° angle to the scroll. You can use this scroll like a headpin. We will make a couple of these scrolls to use in the Donut Wraps on pages 34–38.

Chapter Four

BASIC WIREWORK PROJECTS

Okay. Now that you know the basic moves, it's time to make some stuff. I hope the projects in this chapter provide the beginnings of great things to come for your newfound wireworking skills.

Donut Wraps

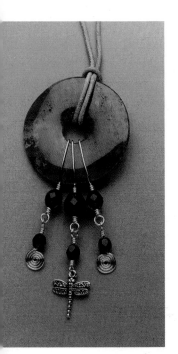

Here's a simple way to add some beautiful wirework to an otherwise dull-looking donut pendant.

For this project, you'll need

20 gauge (0.8mm) half-hard round wire

one donut (anything around 30mm to 50mm will work great)

two scroll headpins (see pages 30–31)

three 6mm beads, two 8mm beads, one 10mm bead

one casting with a loop to hang from the bottom

one yard of leather (or other suitable) cord

two cord ends (to connect your clasp to the leather)

one hook and eye clasp (instructions are covered on pages 74–76)

chain nose pliers

flush cutters

1 Start with a 6" piece of wire, pulled straight. String the donut onto it so that about ⅓ sticks out the top and ⅔ hangs out the bottom.

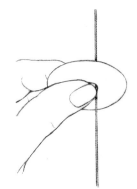

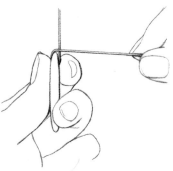

2 Pull the wire ends up over the sides of the donut so that they are parallel to each other.

3 Pull the long end over the top of the donut so that it intersects the short end.

4 Use chain nose pliers to grasp the long end and bend it back up and away from the top of the donut. The long wire curves halfway over the top of the donut and then bends straight up away from it.

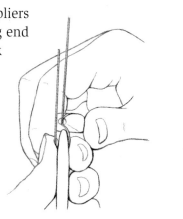

6 Firmly holding down both pieces of wire, wrap the short wire four times around the long wire. Snip the tail of the remaining short wire and tweak the end of the last wrap down (just the way we did for wrapped loops on pages 26–27).

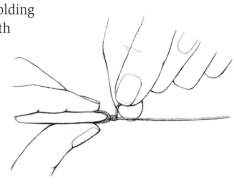

5 Pull the short end over the top of the donut so that it intersects the long end.

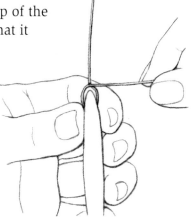

7 String an 8mm bead onto the long piece of wire and make a 90° bend as far away from the bead as needed to make four wraps (see steps 6 and 7 of wrapped loops on page 27).

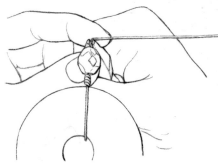

8 Make a wrapped loop, pulling the wraps back up to the bead. Snip the tail off and tweak the end of the last wrap down.

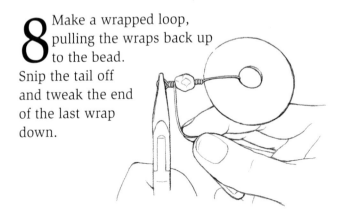

10 Hold the loop of the scroll headpin in your chain nose pliers (which are in your non-dominant hand) as shown. The whole donut mess is hanging off to the left and the headpin is out to the right. Wrap back up to the bead, snip off the tail of wire, and tweak the end of the last wrap down.

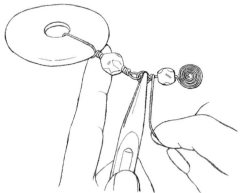

9 String one 6mm bead onto a scroll headpin (see pages 30–31). Make a 90° bend as far away from the bead as needed to make four wraps. Make a loop and connect it to the loop hanging off the donut.

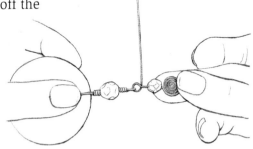

You've now finished one "donut dangle." Repeat steps 1–10 to make another. These will be the "outside" dangles. The center dangle starts off the same way, but you'll hang the 10mm bead on the first wrap, and proceed as follows.

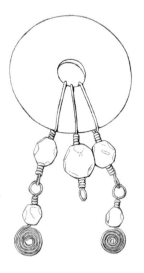

11 Cut a 6" piece of wire. Connect a wrapped loop to the bottom of the wrap with the 10mm bead on it.

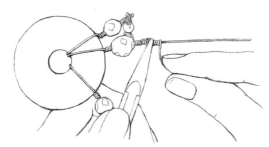

Wrap back up to the 6mm bead, snip the tail off, tweak the end down, and you're done with the dangles.

12 String a 6mm bead onto this wire, connect your casting, and make another wrapped loop, remembering to connect the casting after you've formed the loop but before you start wrapping.

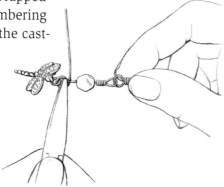

You can now string the donut onto the leather cord as follows.

13 Fold the leather cord in half, forming a hairpin turn in the center.

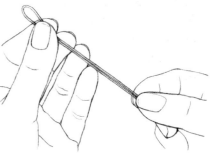

14 Push this loop of leather through the front of the donut so that it comes out the back.

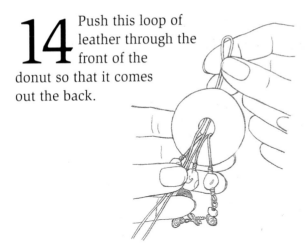

15 Pass the loose ends through the loop and pull tight.

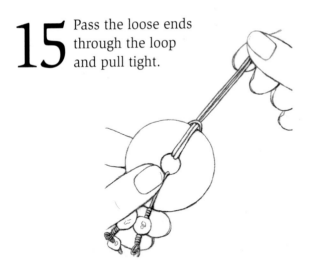

16 Adjust the cord to desired length and attach a clasp with cord ends.

Donut Embellishment

ere's another way to embellish plain donut pendants. This technique was shown to me by my friend Kate Ferrant-Richbourg whose work appears on pages 115–116 of the gallery section.

For this project, you'll need

20 gauge (0.8mm) half-hard round wire

one donut (anything around 30mm to 50mm)

an assortment of 4mm to 8mm beads

one yard of leather (or other suitable) cord

two cord ends (to connect your clasp to the leather)

one hook and eye clasp (instructions are covered on pages 74–76)

chain nose pliers

flush cutters

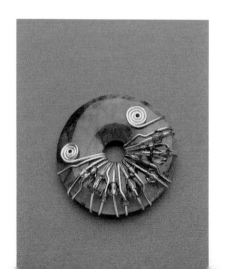

1 Start with a 24" piece of wire, pulled straight. String the donut onto it so that about 3" of wire sticks out through the front of the donut and the rest hangs out the back.

2 Hold the 3" piece of wire down onto the front of the donut with your thumb. Pull the long piece of wire down the back, around to the front, and through the front of the donut.

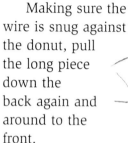

Making sure the wire is snug against the donut, pull the long piece down the back again and around to the front.

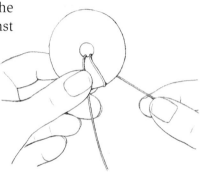

3 String a bead onto the wire and put it through the hole again so that the bead lies on the front of the donut. Pull the wire snug against the donut. Repeat this step, adding a bead to each new wrap, until you're left with about 6" of wire.

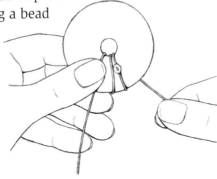

4 Wrap the wire around the donut one more time without a bead, ending with the wire on the front of the donut. Snip both ends of wire down to about 2".

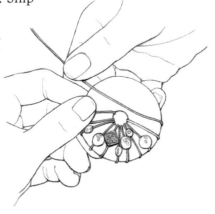

5 Make flat scrolls with these 2" ends of wire.

Finish by stringing the donut onto your cord and attaching a clasp with cord ends as described for the Donut Wrap on page 38.

"Jetson" Earrings

You can create some interesting (if not downright startling) effects in your work by incorporating freeform coils. The techniques are simple.

For this project, you'll need

20 gauge (0.8mm) half-hard round wire

⁵⁄₁₆" (8mm) dowel or pen with a round shaft (not octagonal)

eight 4mm beads

two 8mm beads

two 2" (or longer) headpins

ear wires (don't jump ahead yet, but you'll be able to make your own soon. See pages 60–62)

round nose pliers

chain nose pliers

flush cutters

1 Start with a 12" piece of wire, pulled straight.

2 Holding the dowel (or pen) in your non-dominant hand, place the wire on top of it at a 90° angle. The wire should be placed so that about 1" is pointing towards you, and the rest goes away from you.

3 Hold the wire down on top of the dowel with the thumb of your non-dominant hand. With your dominant hand, grasp the far end of the wire and begin wrapping it around the dowel. Keeping the wire and dowel perpendicular to each other while wrapping, continue until you've used the entire length of wire. The coil will form onto the dowel from left to right if you're right-handed and from right to left if you're left-handed.

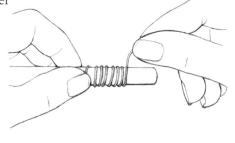

4 Slide the coil off the dowel and look down the length of it. The whole coil should be nice and round except for one tail sticking out from each end. Snip off the two tails.

5 Hold the coil between the index finger and thumb of your non-dominant hand (as if you are saying "okay" with it in your fingers). Make sure that the last loop does not extend past your fingertips. Turn the coil so the very end is halfway between your index finger and thumb.

6 Using round nose pliers, make a small P with the very tip of the wire toward the inside of the coil. This small loop should form in the middle of your thumb.

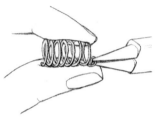

7 Hold the coil so you can look down through the inside and turn it so that the small loop you've just made is on top, at 12 o'clock.

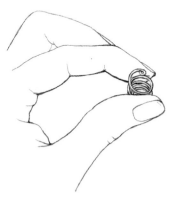

8 Place flush cutters at 3 o'clock on the fourth coil down and snip.

9 Put the snipped-off piece of coil aside for the moment and hold the coil with the loop in the "okay" position so that the cut end is near your fingertips as in Step 5. Put another small **P** in this end. To finish off, grasp both small **P**s with your fingers and pull the coil apart slightly so the entire length is about ¾".

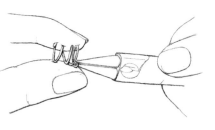

10 The end loops should be opposite each other (one at 12 o'clock, the other at 6 o'clock). If they aren't, you probably didn't cut the coil at 3 o'clock in Step 8 and you'll have to start over.

11 Here's the fun part. String a 4mm bead onto a headpin. Put the headpin through the small loop at one end of the coil, go through the coil, and come out the other end without going through the second small loop.

12 String a 4mm bead, an 8mm bead, and another 4mm bead onto the headpin. These three beads go inside the coil. You may have to pull the coil open a little to get the 8mm bead in there.

13 Push the headpin through the small loop in the other end of the coil, then string a 4mm bead onto the end.

14 Grasp the top of the head-pin (right where it comes out of the last 4mm bead) with chain nose pliers. Gently push the beads and coil together so there are no spaces between them.

15 Holding the last 4mm bead steady with your index finger, make a 90° bend sideways, away from your index finger.

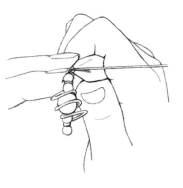

16 Snip the excess wire off and make a perfect loop (see pages 20–21) in the top. Attach an ear wire to the loop using the method for opening loops discussed on page 23.

Now make another earring so you have a pair. Use the coil set aside in Step 9.

Chapter Five

FINDINGS

Findings are jewelry parts that are used to attach something to a chain, bracelet, or ear wire. The findings in this chapter will allow you to turn a prized crystal drop into a pendant or make earrings out of just about anything.

5 Pull the other wire over the top of the crystal so that it crosses the shaft of wire you are going to place a wrap on. This is the tail of wire you are going to wrap with.

6 Hold the top of the crystal so that you are firmly holding down both pieces of wire, and wrap the tail two or three times around the shaft.

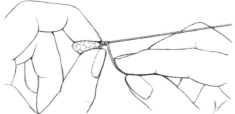

7 Snip off the remaining tail and tweak the end of the last wrap down (same as for wrapped loops on pages 24–29). Make a 90° bend in the shaft.

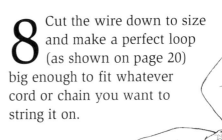

8 Cut the wire down to size and make a perfect loop (as shown on page 20) big enough to fit whatever cord or chain you want to string it on.

Fancy Headpins

Headpins are about the most pedestrian of jewelry findings. They are simply a short piece of wire with a small nailhead at one end. A bead or beads are strung on the pin and a loop is made in the plain end. That loop is then attached to the bottom of an earring or whatever. These fancy headpins are interesting alternatives to plain ones. All the fancy headpins shown here start out with scrolls, which we covered on pages 30–31. Please go back and review this section if you are unsure how to proceed.

To make headpins you'll need

20 gauge (0.8mm) half-hard round wire

round nose pliers

chain nose pliers

flat nose pliers

flush cutters

Triangle Headpin

Most of the bends you'll need to form the points of the triangle are made with your hands. Use the chain nose pliers as a form over which you pull the wire.

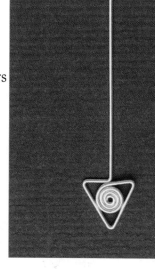

1 Start with a 6" piece of wire, pulled straight.

2 Start a flat scroll as explained on pages 30–31. Stop scrolling when you've completed three revolutions.

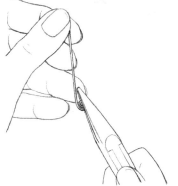

3 Position the wire so that it is horizontal in front of you with the scroll on top and at one end.

4 Grasp the wire with your chain nose as shown, and "fold" the wire up onto the scroll. This is the first point of the triangle. Slide the pliers so they are flush up against the scroll.

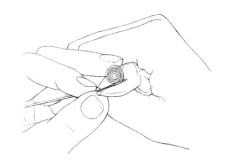

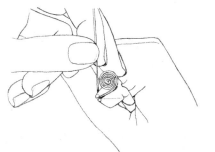

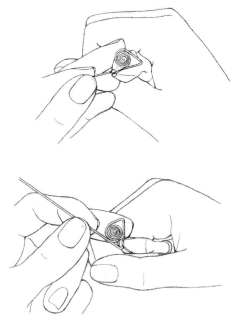

5 Hold the piece of wire again as shown, and repeat Step 4. This is the second point of the triangle.

6 Hold the piece of wire as shown and repeat Step 4. This is the third point of the triangle.

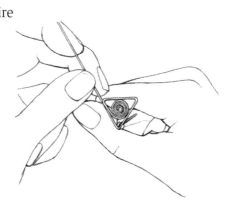

7 Now that the triangle is formed, you'll need to make one last bend. Imagine a line that runs from the top point of the triangle through the center of the scroll. Grasp the wire with your flat nose pliers just past the center point, and pull the wire back away from the triangle to a 90° angle.

Heart Headpin

The only real difference between this headpin and the triangle headpin is that two of the points are made with round nose pliers instead of chain nose. Once again, the pliers are used as a form onto which the wire is pulled.

1 Start with a 6" piece of wire, pulled straight.

2 Start a flat scroll, as explained on pages 30–31. Stop scrolling when you've completed three revolutions.

3 Position the wire so that it is horizontal in front of you with the scroll on top and at one end.

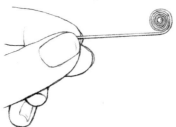

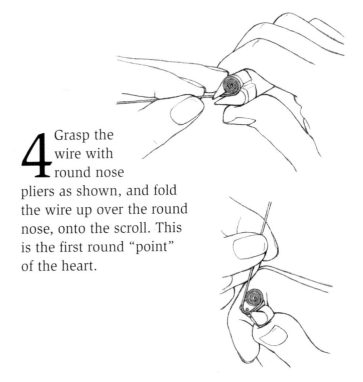

4 Grasp the wire with round nose pliers as shown, and fold the wire up over the round nose, onto the scroll. This is the first round "point" of the heart.

5 Hold the piece of wire again as shown in Step 4. Repeat Step 4, only this time use chain nose pliers. This is the bottom point of the heart.

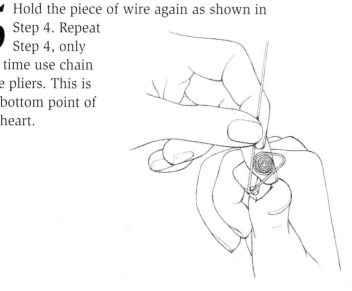

6 Hold the piece of wire again as in Step 4. Repeat Step 4, using the round nose again. This is the second (and last) round point of your heart. Try to form both round points of the heart at the same place on your round nose pliers so that the heart looks even.

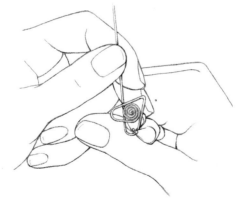

7 Once the heart is formed, you'll need to make one last bend. Grasp the wire with your chain nose pliers just above the intersection of the beginning and ending of your heart. Pull the wire up and away from the scroll inside the heart.

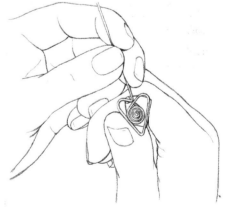

Star Headpins

The trick here is to visualize a five-pointed star while you are making the bends. The bends that form the points of the star are made with your hands. Use the chain nose pliers as a form onto which the wire is pulled.

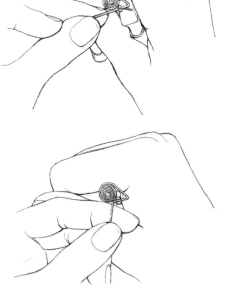

1 Start with a 6" piece of wire, pulled straight.

2 Start a scroll as before, and stop scrolling when you've completed three revolutions.

3 Position the wire so that it is horizontal in front of you with the scroll on top and at one end.

Grasp the wire with your chain nose as shown, and fold the wire up onto the scroll. This is the first point of the star.

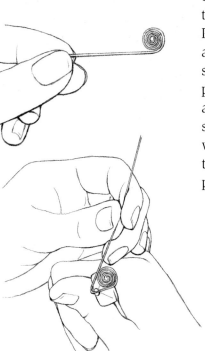

4 Here's where visualization comes into play. Imagine a five-pointed star, starting with the one point in front of you. Reposition the scroll and grasp the wire with one tip of the chain nose in the first point. Pull the wire away from the scroll, onto the pliers to the angle (are you visualizing it?) at which you need to start the next point of the star.

5 Place the chain nose up against the scroll on the other side of the bend and pull the wire back onto the scroll.

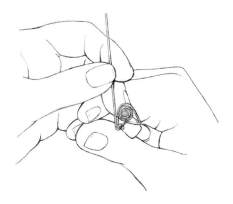

6 Continue bending points as described above until the last point is completed. Finish the headpin by bending the wire straight down, away from the star.

Chapter Six

EAR WIRES

Have you ever wished for ear wires
that look like more than necessary hardware
bought through some hand-drawn mail-order
catalog? Wish no more. You are about to learn
how to make fantastic ear wires for just about
any occasion. Even better, you'll be able to make
them out of just about anything!

In general, I recommend 20 gauge (0.8 mm) wire for ear wires. The 22 gauge (0.6 mm) is too small and flimsy to withstand the wear and tear that most earrings receive, and 18 gauge (1.0 mm) is too thick to poke through your ear lobe (alternative body piercing notwithstanding).

The most important tool for making ear wires isn't some expensive jig or new high-tech pliers. The best piece of equipment I have found to make ear wires is a regular old ball-point pen. The pen has to have a round shaft (not octagonal) and it shouldn't be too wide. (I use the BIC Softfeel™ pen—the smooth rubber coating really grips!)

In my experience, probably half the infections that people get in their earlobes from ear wires are *not* because they are allergic to the metal. The problem is usually caused by ear wire ends that are really rough or have very sharp sides. These ends make small scrapes in your ears, and the scrapes become aggravated or infected by the ear wire passing over and rubbing them.

You can solve this problem by simply taking the time to file the points of your ear wires smooth. You can do this with a flat file, but a cup burr yields the best results. A cup burr looks like a small drill bit except that its very tip is actually scooped out into a tiny cup with small teeth. You can use a cup burr with any Dremel™ tool or Flex-Shaft™ drill. All you need to do is put the end of your ear wire into the cup, turn the tool on, and the burr files the end into a beautiful little dome that can be put through any ear-piercing without worry of scrapes. When you're buying (or ordering) a cup burr, select a burr that is two gauge sizes bigger than your wire. For example, if you are using 20-gauge (0.8 mm) wire, you want to use an 18-gauge (1.0 mm) cup burr. The large cup burr makes it easy to get the wire into that impossibly small cup!

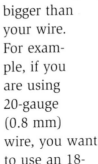

When you're filing ends down with a needle file, start by filing the very tip flat (keep the flat edge of the file perpendicular to the wire). Once the end is

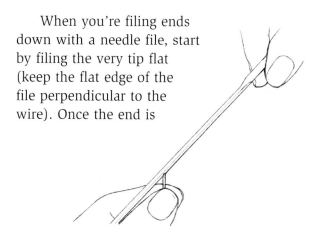

nice and flat, file at a 45° angle along the sides of the tip so there are no sharp edges.

It's a good idea to hammer the front side of the ear wire flat. Hammering has a two-fold effect; it hardens the wire so your ear wire will stand up to daily wear and tear, and it is

aesthetically pleasing when done correctly. Be sure not to flatten the part of the ear wire that slides into your ear; only the front of the ear wire from the top down to the loop (or bead) should be flattened.

When you're using a hammer, try to keep the face of the hammer flush with the bench block. Otherwise you'll get lots of little dints in the flat part of your ear wire. Let the weight of the hammer do most of the work. All you have to do is keep the face flush with your bench block, and guide the hammer so you don't whack your fingers.

Plain Ear Wires

For this project you'll need

20 gauge (0.8mm) half-hard round wire

round nose pliers

chain nose pliers

flush cutters

pen

needle file or cup burr and Dremel tool

bench block and hammer

1 Cut a 3" piece of wire and pull it straight.

2 Make a small perfect loop (as shown on page 20) in one end. Make this loop near the tip of your round nose pliers.

3 Hold the wire in the very tip of your round nose pliers, right up against the bend of the loop.

4 Pull the wire over your pliers to almost a 90° angle.

5 Grasp the loop in your non-dominant hand, between the tips of your index finger and thumb, so that the long piece of wire that comes out of the loop is pointing toward you.

6 Hold the pen in your dominant hand and position the wire between your thumb and the pen as shown.

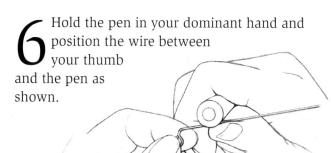

7 Place the pen on top of the wire about ½" away from the bend and roll the wire around the pen until the big loop you are making is centered over the small loop you first made.

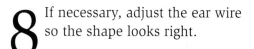

8 If necessary, adjust the ear wire so the shape looks right.

9 Cut off the excess wire about ¼" past the bottom of the small loop.

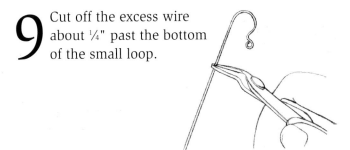

10 Make a slight bend away from the loop with the last ¼" of wire.

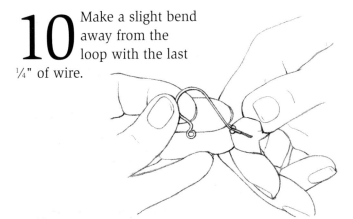

11 File the tip and hammer the front of the ear wire as described at the beginning of this section. The best way to position the ear wire on the bench block for hammering is to hang it off the side. This way, there is no chance of accidentally hammering parts of the ear wire that you want to keep round, and as you'll see in a minute, there's no way you will accidentally smash a bead you've worked into it.

Plain Ear Wires with a Bead

This is a plain ear wire with a bead added.

For this project you'll need

20 gauge (0.8mm) half-hard round wire

round nose pliers

chain nose pliers

flush cutters

pen

needle file or cup burr and Dremel tool

bench block and hammer

small (4mm) bead

1 Cut a 3" piece of wire and pull it straight.

2 Make a small perfect loop in one end as described on page 20.

3 Slide the small bead onto the wire, right up against the loop. Holding the loop and bead with the tips of your fingers, pull the wire over to almost a 90° angle. It may actually help if you anchor the top of the bead and pull the wire over onto your thumbnail.

4 Now grasp the bead with your non-dominant hand, between the tips of your index finger and thumb, so that the long piece of wire that comes out of the bead is pointing toward you.

5 Hold the pen in your dominant hand and position the wire between your thumb and the pen as shown.

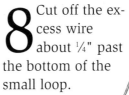

8 Cut off the excess wire about ¼" past the bottom of the small loop.

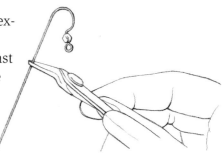

6 Position the pen about ½" away from the bend and roll the wire around the pen until the big loop you are making is centered over the bead.

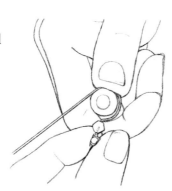

9 Make a slight bend away from the loop with the last ¼" of wire.

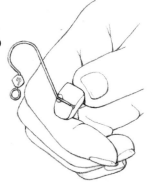

7 Adjust the ear wire so the shape looks right.

10 File the tip and hammer the front of the ear wire as described in the plain ear wire section. Remember to hang the ear wire off the side of the bench block. This way, there is no chance of accidentally smashing the bead into oblivion.

Fancy Ear Wires

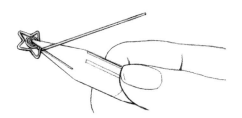

Now that you've seen how easy it is to make your own ear wires, a little practice will open many new possibilities. You can make an ear wire out of just about anything. For instance, go back and make a few fancy headpins as described on pages 49 through 55. If you bend the long piece of wire coming from the shape to almost ninety degrees, you can work it as described above and have ear wires like you've never seen before!

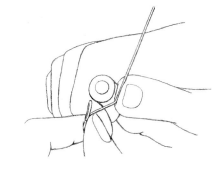

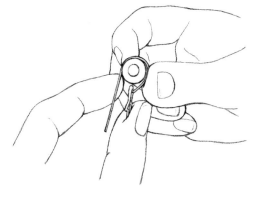

Chapter Seven

CLASPS

You can construct many types of clasps with wirework techniques, and just about any rudimentary loop and hook arrangement can be called a clasp. Clasps can also be big elaborate flowing curves of metal adorned with beads and touches of wire. In essence, though, most wire clasps are a variation on one of two different themes: the **S** clasp, or the hook and eye clasp. The major difference between these two is that the **S** clasp is only one piece (usually hooked through jump rings attached to each end of the necklace or bracelet), and the hook and eye clasp is two pieces (attached to either end of the necklace or bracelet).

S Clasps

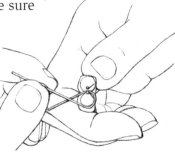

All of these **S** clasps use 18 gauge (1.0mm) half-hard round wire in their construction. Some of the fancier ones we'll be making later will also use some 20 gauge (0.8mm) wire, but 18 gauge wire generally yields stronger clasps. This big wire is a lot more fun to hammer than the 20 gauge because you can really whack it into beautiful flat curves that almost look like cast metal pieces when finished. Hammering the bigger curves in your clasps will really harden the wire to help secure even the heaviest necklaces.

The Classic S Clasp

This is a very basic clasp. I actually like to use this clasp (made slightly smaller than shown here) as a chain link. A whole bracelet of these is visually very stunning, but we're not here to make chains (maybe that will be another book!).

For this clasp you'll need

18 gauge (1.0mm) half-hard round wire

round nose pliers

chain nose pliers

flush cutters

bench block and hammer

1 Start with a 3" piece of wire, pulled straight.

2 Grasp the wire about 1" from the end, in the fattest part of your round nose pliers.

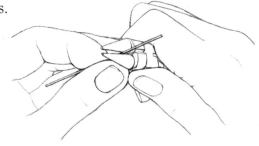

3 Start bending the wire into a loop away from you until the 1" end of wire comes all the way around and crosses itself at about a 135° angle to make a kind of teardrop shape. Make sure that the short piece of wire that is now angled down is nearest the hand holding the pliers.

4 Hold the loop between your index finger and thumb, and turn the ends of wire so that the short piece is angled up and the long piece is angled down.

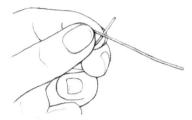

5 Grasp the long piece of wire in the fattest part of your round nose pliers about ½" away from the intersection.

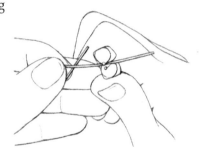

6 Ideally, the loops in either end of the clasp will be equidistant from the intersection. Start to roll the wire up over the pliers, but stop when the partially formed loop is the same distance away from the intersection as the first one.

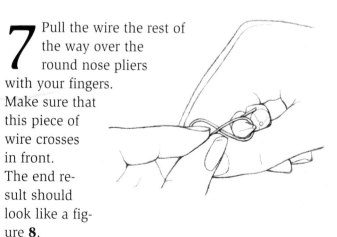

7 Pull the wire the rest of the way over the round nose pliers with your fingers. Make sure that this piece of wire crosses in front. The end result should look like a figure **8**.

8 Snip the ends of the wires down to ¼" past the intersection.

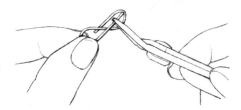

9 Using the round nose pliers, make a small **P** in both ends of wire so that the loops are on the outside of the clasp. You'll need to do this by pulling one loop towards you, the other one away from you.

10 Hammer the big curves almost flat. Hang the clasp off the side of the bench block so that the small loops in the center of the clasp are not against the block and in danger of being flattened. Actually, you can hammer this just about any way you want, but I find that having only the big sweeping round parts of the clasp flattened looks best.

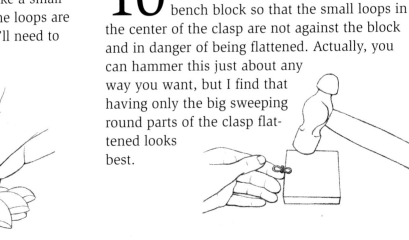

You may notice that when you hammer your clasp, it begins to open up. Don't worry, this is a normal reaction of the wire being flattened. All you need to do is pull the loop closed after you're done hammering.

As previously mentioned, these **S** clasps attach to a necklace or bracelet via jump rings at either end.

S Clasp with a Bead

This clasp is a little more interesting than the plain **S**. We'll use two different gauges of wire: 18 gauge (1.0mm) for the clasp, and 20 gauge (0.8mm) for the embellishment. Once you've made a few of these, you can adjust the size and make them huge or small. I've seen these clasps made impossibly huge, but used wisely (as in the side of a necklace as a featured component) they can be quite striking. For the clasp we will make here, try using a nice firepolished crystal or an interesting 8mm bead.

For this clasp you'll need

18 gauge (1.0mm) half-hard round wire

20 gauge (0.8mm) half-hard round wire

one 8mm bead

round nose pliers

chain nose pliers

flush cutters

bench block and hammer

pen (like the one described for making ear wires on page 58)

1 Start with a 5" piece of 18 gauge wire and a 6" piece of 20 gauge wire, both pulled straight.

2 Hold the 18 gauge wire in your non-dominant hand, and place the 20 gauge wire on top of and perpendicular to the 18 gauge piece. Hold the pieces together between your thumb and index finger with your thumb on top.

3 Make three nice tight wraps of the 20 gauge wire around the 18 gauge piece. Slide the bead onto the 18 gauge wire and hold it tightly against the wrap.

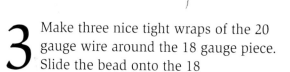

4 Holding the bead firmly, wrap the wire around the bead. For the best effect, go completely around the outside of the bead at least once. Finish by wrapping tightly twice on the other side of the bead.

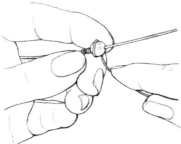

5 Snip the two little tails off the ends of the wraps and slide the bead and wire wrap into the middle of the 18 gauge piece of wire. Tweak the ends of the wraps down.

6 Make the big side loops as for the classic **S** clasp, but do so with a pen rather than round nose pliers. These loops should cross the center wire just in front of the wire wraps on either side of the bead.

7 Snip the ends of the wires down to ¼" past the intersections.

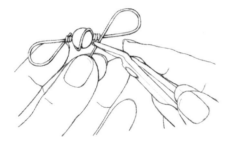

8 Using round nose pliers, make a small **P** in both ends of wire so that the loops are on the outside of the clasp. You'll need to do this by pulling one loop toward you, the other one away from you.

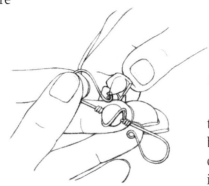

9 Hammer the big curves almost flat. Hang the clasp off the side of the bench block so that the bead isn't on the block and in danger of being smashed into dust.

Variations on this **S** clasp are endless and you can make some pretty outstanding pieces. Try using big glass hearts, funky pressed glass shapes, or anything you think will work.

Hook and Eye Clasps

Variations of hook and eye clasps have been used in jewelry for centuries. While some are slightly less decorative than the large **S** clasp with beads (see page 71), you can make other hook and eye clasps that are just as fancy. The beauty of these clasps is that they are very easy to use, they are very secure, and they are relatively easy to make. The clasps shown here are made with either 18 or 20 gauge wire. Which wire you choose depends on what kind of clasp you are going to make. A hook and eye clasp made from a single piece of wire works just fine with 18 gauge wire. Using a doubled-over piece of wire for a clasp is much easier with 20 gauge, and is still very strong.

The Classic Hook and Eye Clasp

The first clasp shown here is just a regular hook and eye. We'll be using 18 gauge wire for this one because it's much sturdier (especially when hammered) than 20 gauge. The hook is fairly simple, and the eye is really just a small figure eight.

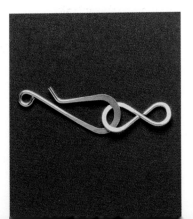

For this clasp you'll need

18 gauge half-hard round wire

round nose pliers

chain nose pliers

flush cutters

bench block and hammer

pen (like the one described for making ear wires on page 58)

The Hook

1 Start with a 3" piece of wire, pulled straight.

2 Make a large teardrop-shaped loop with your pen (same as for the **S** clasp, page 68) about 1" from one end. Pull this loop all the way around until it crosses itself at a 135° angle.

3 Bend the tip of wire that extends past the intersection back up so you create a kind of elbow in the wire. The elbow rests on the longer piece of wire.

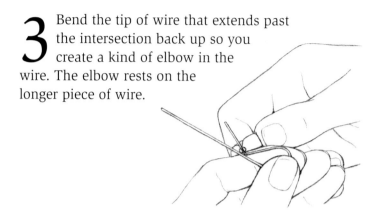

4 Snip the tip of wire to ¼", just past the elbow.

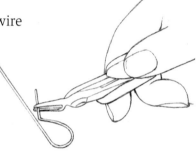

6 Make a **P** with the end you've just snipped, pulling it away from and onto the back of the big loop.

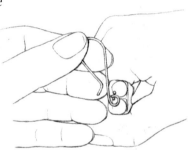

5 Turn the hook around and snip the other end down to about ½" past the tip.

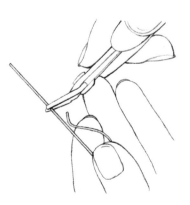

7 Hammer the hook almost flat. You can either flatten just the round parts of this clasp, or the whole thing. I think it looks best when the whole length is flattened.

The Eye

1 Start with a 3" piece of wire, pulled straight.

Follow the directions for the Classic **S** clasp (pages 68–70), with the following exceptions.

2 Grasp the wire at not quite the fattest part of the round nose pliers.

3 Make the figure **8** a lot rounder. Pull the wire around and make the two end pieces cross each other at more than the 135° angle used in the **S** clasp.

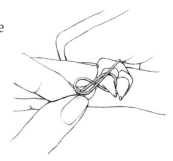

4 Snip both ends right at the intersection so they sit flush up against it.

5 Hammer the eye flat. When you are hammering the eye flat, the loops will more than likely open slightly. Just pull them closed with the round nose pliers. Attach the eye to the hook.

Strongest Wire Hook and Eye Clasp in the Universe

I love this clasp. It is one of the most versatile, easily-made wire clasps, yet it is among the strongest. The reason for its strength lies in the fact that the hook and the eye are each made from one piece of wire. Both ends of each piece are also at the end of nice, tight wraps, which adds even more security.

For this clasp you'll need

20 gauge half-hard round wire

round nose pliers

chain nose pliers

flush cutters

The Hook

Because the hook uses one piece of wire that is bent over into a double wire, it is very important that you pull the wire into a very straight length to begin with.

1 Start with a 6" piece of wire, pulled as straight as you can make it.

2 Using your chain nose pliers, bend the first two inches into a nice, sharp 90° bend.

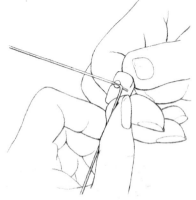

3 With your fingers, push the bend all the way closed to create a hairpin turn. Using your chain nose pliers, push the two sides together lightly, forcing them closed near the top of the hairpin.

4 Orient the wire so that the hairpin is at the top, the shorter of the two ends of wire is on the right, and the longer end is on the left. Using round nose pliers, make a tiny **P** at the top of the hairpin—bend both sides of the hairpin into this **P** using the very tip of your pliers and bending away from you.

5 Now, turn the hairpin around so the tiny **P** is facing toward you. Grasp the hairpin about ¼" down from the **P** with the widest part of your round nose pliers.

Bend away from you until the back of the **P** meets what will be the inside of the clasp.

6 Snip the shorter of the two ends of wire about ⅜" from the **P**.

7 Using the chain nose pliers, grasp the longer piece of wire so that the pliers are right up against the shorter piece. Bend the longer piece away from the shorter piece at a 90° angle.

8 Hold the clasp in your non-dominant hand so the longer piece you've just bent is pointing towards you, and hold the round nose pliers in your other hand with your palm facing out. Grasp the wire about ¼" away from the bend. Start to loop the wire up and over by rolling the pliers away from you. Be sure the wire and pliers are perpendicular to each other. Stop looping when one of two things happens: First, imagine that the loop is complete. If the imagined completed loop is centered over the wire, stop bending. Or, when you get to the point that, if you were to continue rolling you'd pull out the bend you made in Step 7, stop bending. Now pull the wire the rest of the way around onto the round nose pliers so you've completed a loop, and the tail end of wire is perpendicular to the bottom of your clasp.

9 Holding the chain nose pliers in your non-dominant hand, grasp the loop you just made, and wrap the tail end of wire around both pieces of wire in the clasp. Make three or four tight wraps, ending the last wrap flat on the inside of the clasp.

Snip the tail off and tweak it down onto the clasp with your chain nose pliers.

The Eye

1 Start with a 6" piece of wire, pulled more or less straight.

2 Using your round nose pliers, grasp the wire ½" away from the top and bend it all the way around until the wire has crossed itself at a 135° angle.

3 Holding the inside of the loop at the intersection, pull both ends down and out slightly so they become parallel to each other and the whole thing looks kind of like a cotter pin.

4 Snip the shorter end off ¼" from the bend.

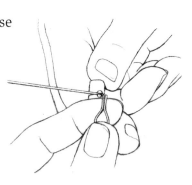

5 Using chain nose pliers, grasp the longer piece of wire and slide your pliers right up against the shorter piece. Bend the longer piece away from the shorter piece at a 90° angle.

6 Hold the eye so the longer piece you've just bent is pointing toward you and make a wrapped loop, just like the one described in Steps 8 and 9 of the hook section. This time, however, continue wrapping until you reach the bends where the two wires separate (probably 7 or 8 wraps).

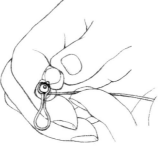

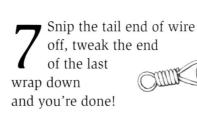

7 Snip the tail end of wire off, tweak the end of the last wrap down and you're done!

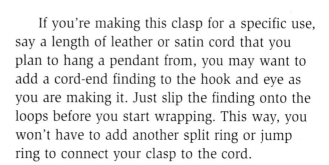

If you're making this clasp for a specific use, say a length of leather or satin cord that you plan to hang a pendant from, you may want to add a cord-end finding to the hook and eye as you are making it. Just slip the finding onto the loops before you start wrapping. This way, you won't have to add another split ring or jump ring to connect your clasp to the cord.

The most critical aspect of building a cage into a pendant is the collar. The collar is formed by all the wire bars of the cage drawn up on top and built into a loop through which you can string a chain or other cord. Making a collar can be tricky, except that I have developed a technique that employs crimp forming pliers. To my knowledge, very few people use this technique, but it is so simple and effective that I'm sure many wireworkers will use it in the future.

A cage also needs to keep your stone, marble, whatever, firmly in the pendant. By holding sections of the bars together with small wire wraps, we can effectively cut off any means of escape for your treasure. Where you would put these wraps depends entirely on the shape of your stone (not to mention your own creative juices).

have a suitable dowel, you can use anything with the right diameter: a seed bead vial, one of those thick hi-liter pens, or, with a little finesse, you can even use the marble itself. The trick is to pull the bars of the cage into the shape you want, arrange them into the pendant loop, and fix the marble inside.

For a marble cage you'll need

20 gauge (0.8mm) half-hard round wire

round nose pliers

chain nose pliers

flush cutters

crimp forming pliers

flat nose pliers

a marble (approximately 14mm looks really nice)

a wooden dowel (approximately the same size as, or with a diameter slightly larger than, your marble)

a rubber band, (one of those thick ones that newspaper carriers or postal workers use)

a pen (one that will leave marks on the wire, such as a fine point Sharpie™)

Wirewrapping Marbles

Cages for marbles are formed around the outside of a wooden dowel. Ideally, you'll use a dowel that has the same diameter (or a slightly larger one) as your marble. If you don't

1 Cut three pieces of wire as follows: two 8" pieces and one 3" piece. Pull them straight.

2 Hold the chain nose pliers in your non-dominant hand, with the tips pointing straight out in front of you.

3 Line up both 8" pieces of wire and grasp them with the chain nose pliers. Leave about 2" of wire hanging out the side toward the back of your hand.

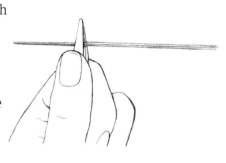

4 Place the 3" piece of wire on top of the chain nose pliers, sticking straight out toward the tips and angled slightly toward the long ends of the 8" pieces. Hold the wire on top of the pliers with your thumb.

5 Grasp the other end of the 3" piece and wrap it tightly around the two 8" pieces 3 times.

6 The last wrap should end up on the front side of the 8" pieces. The tail at the beginning of the wrap will come off the same side of the 8" pieces.

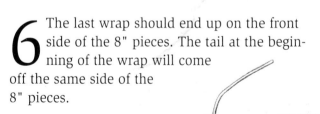

7 Snip both tails of wire off the ends of the wrap. At this stage it's important to have flush cutters that come to a very small point at the tip. Get into the small space just past where the wrap comes up and over the 8" pieces of wire and snip the tail off so that it lies more or less in between the two 8" pieces.

8 Slide the binding wrap so that it is about 2" away from one end of the 8" pieces. Carefully tweak the ends of the wraps down onto the 8" pieces so they hold tightly (don't smash them down flat, just gently coax them into place).

9 Hold the dowel in your non-dominant hand and place the binding wrap you've just made so that the cut tail ends are against the dowel and all you see on the outside are the three nice tight wraps.

10 Holding the wrap down with your thumb, pull both sets of wires over the dowel until they cross each other directly opposite the binding wrap and run off in opposite directions.

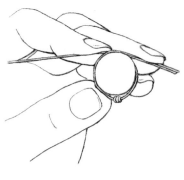

11 Holding everything in place, draw a small line across all four pieces of wire directly opposite the wrap. I'm going to say it again: It's very important that these marks are directly opposite the binding wrap. The distance from the binding wrap to these marks must be exactly the same on both sets of wires.

12 Pull the cage off the dowel. Using the pen marks as guides, pull both sets of wires up and away from the loop so that the bends are just about 90° angles. Ideally, the four wires will line up flush when you pull both sets closed.

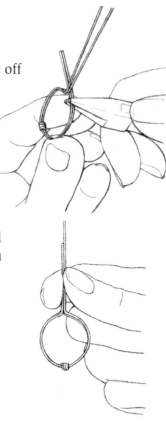

14 Bend the remaining long piece of wire sideways, away from the other to not quite 90°.

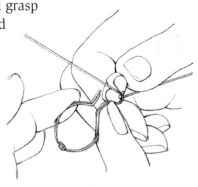

13 You should now have four pieces of wire sticking straight out of the top of the cage: two short ones and two long ones. Snip the two shorter wires down to ¼" and bend one of the longer wires to a nice sharp 90° angle as shown. The bend has to be exactly ¼" away from the loop, flush with the two smaller ends you've just snipped.

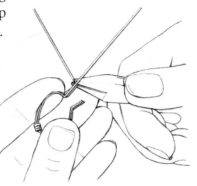

15 Make a wrapped loop with the first piece of wire you made the 90° bend in. Hold the loop with the long piece of wire pointing toward you, your palm out, and grasp the wire with round nose pliers about ¼" away from the bend. Then form the loop just like the wrapped loops on pages 24–26.

16 Using the outside station of crimp forming pliers, gather all four pieces of wire coming off the loop and hold the pliers closed. The crimping pliers should be placed right up against the shoulder of the cage, angled down and away from the loop in the top of the collar. Wrap a rubber band three or four times around the handles of the pliers to keep them held closed. You can now work with both hands while the crimping pliers hold everything together.

Here's where it gets a little bit tricky.

17 Holding the chain nose pliers in your non-dominant hand and sticking straight out in front of you, grasp the loop you've made in the top of the collar.

18 Pull the wire from your wrapped loop around *all four* pieces of wire that are being held together by the crimping pliers. Start wrapping slowly, forming nice, even, perpendicular, and most importantly tight wraps all the way up to the crimping pliers. Pull the wraps most of the way around, until the crimping pliers are in the way, then let go, grasp the wire again from underneath, and repeat. You should end up with at least three or four tight wraps on your collar. *Note:* These wraps should start underneath the last long piece that you bent to not quite 90°.

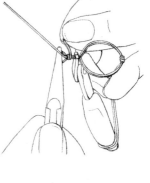

19 Remove the rubber band from the crimping pliers and pull the pliers off the collar. You can now continue pulling nice tight wraps all the way down to the shoulder of the cage. Once you've finished wrapping, snip the end down and tweak it flat onto the collar.

Finishing Off Your Pendant

20 Snip the last piece of wire that bends out of the top of your collar down to about 1½". Using the technique explained on pages 30–31, make a flat scroll perpendicular to the collar. The scroll will be pushed down flat onto the collar later, but for the time being leave it where it is.

21 Put your marble into the loop and pull the pairs of wire apart until they fully quarter the sphere. Don't worry if the marble is loose in the cage; the end result is actually much more striking if it is loose at this point.

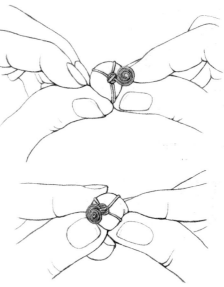

22

To add a little decoration and to tighten the cage around the marble, grasp each of the bars halfway between the binding wrap and the collar in the very tips of flat nose pliers. Twist each bar slightly clockwise to create a zigzag effect and take up the slack until the bars are tight up against the sides of the marble.

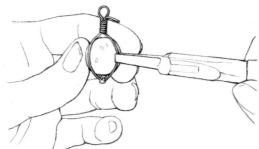

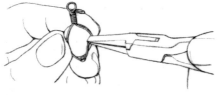

23

Finally, push the flat scroll down onto your collar so it lies perpendicular to the pendant loop you built in the top. This flat scroll will face front and hide the collar.

Wire Capped Bead

Here's a simple project that adds dramatic wirework to otherwise plain old round beads. Perfectly round beads work best with this technique, but faceted firepolished glass beads or slightly uneven semi-precious beads also work. The techniques are fairly straightforward, but the wrapping of the cap demands a colossal amount of finesse; you will be wrapping exceptionally long pieces of wire into scrolls. Any kinks or untoward bends in these long pieces of wire will make them impossible to scroll smoothly, rendering your cap uneven. Hold the wires as close to the ends as possible at all times.

For this project you'll need

20 gauge (0.8mm) half-hard round wire

14mm or larger round bead

nylon jaw wire straightening pliers

chain nose pliers

flush cutters

round nose pliers

1 Cut a piece of wire 28" (yes, that's 2 feet, 4 inches!) long. Using the techniques described on page 17, pull the wire nice and straight, removing any kinks with the nylon jaw pliers. It's important that the wire be straight and kink-free.

2 Make a 90° bend 13" from one end of the wire. Your wire now has two parts; a 13" piece and a 15" piece separated by a bend.

13"

3 You are going to make a wrapped loop (as explained on pages 24–27). With your thumb in the "sacred bend," hold onto the 15" piece, which extends straight down.

4 Make a wrapped loop, but place only two wraps beneath the loop.

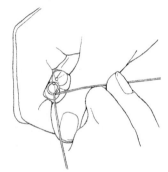

Don't cut the long tail of wire off the end of your wrap! You'll need this piece of wire to make the cap and scroll.

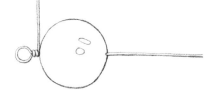

5 String your bead onto the 15" piece of wire, and slide it up to the wrap.

6 Grasp the 15" length of wire coming out of the bead with the very tip of your chain nose pliers, and make a nice sharp 90° bend over and onto the top of the pliers.

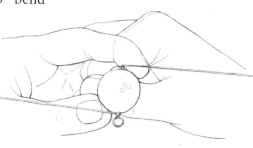

7 When you remove the pliers, there will be a small length of wire between the bead and the bend. This bend is the "sacred bend" on this side of the bead.

Make another wrapped loop on this side, but stop wrapping after 2½ turns.

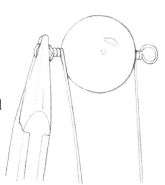

8 Now turn the bead over and place a half wrap on the other side. Repeat this step, alternating sides until you end up with the same number of wraps tight up against the bead on both sides. *Again, don't cut the long tails of wire off the ends of the wraps!*

10 Gently pull the long tail of wire that is coming off the bottom wrap down *slightly*. You only want this wire out of your way momentarily— you don't want to put any kinks or bends in it.

9 Here's where the fun begins. Hold one of the wrapped loops with the chain nose pliers in your non-dominant hand. Orient your pliers so they are parallel to the floor and the bead hangs out the bottom, extending downward.

11 Grasp the end of the piece of wire coming off the wrapped loop you are holding with the pliers. Continue wrapping, angled down ever so slightly, until a wire cap begins to form onto the shoulder of the bead. You should pull the wire only hard enough to get it around onto the cap. If you pull too hard, the cap will bunch up into a nasty wire mess around the wrapped loop. Try to keep your wrapping hand in a very even orbit around the bead.

Stop wrapping when you've got around six wraps in your cap. The cap will spring open slightly. *Don't panic!* This is normal and doesn't take away from the inherent loveliness of the piece. *Don't cut the long tail of wire off the end of the cap.* You'll need this to make the flat scroll that sits on the side of the bead between the two caps.

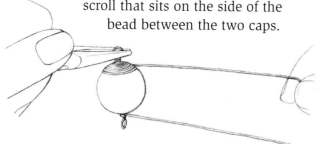

12 Repeat Step 11 on the other side of the bead.

13 To make the flat scrolls that will decorate the sides of your bead, you'll need 2" of wire coming off the two caps. These need to extend off the caps on opposite sides of the bead. You can achieve this by unwrapping one cap slightly, until the two are lined up correctly. The idea is that when you have finished making your flat scrolls, they will lie on opposite sides of the bead.

14 Cut these wires down to the aforementioned 2".

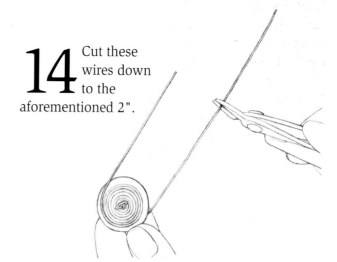

15 Hold onto the bead with one cap facing toward you (imagine that you are looking through the hole in the bead). You will make your flat scroll with the piece of wire coming off this cap first. Using the techniques described on pages 30–31, begin making a flat scroll by rolling (away from you) the tail of wire coming off the cap.

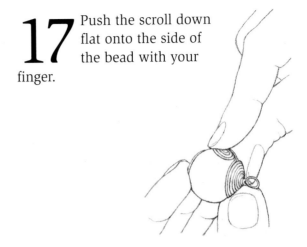

17 Push the scroll down flat onto the side of the bead with your finger.

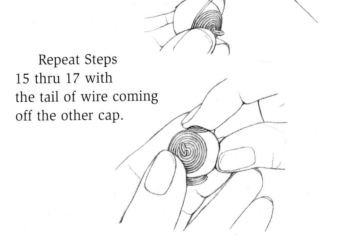

16 Continue until all the wire is used up and your scroll is right up against the cap.

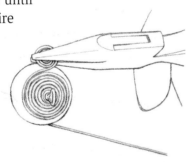

Repeat Steps 15 thru 17 with the tail of wire coming off the other cap.

Wirewrapping Cabochons

The dictionary defines a cabochon as "a highly polished, convex cut, unfaceted gem," but most people tend to use the word to describe any material with the same basic physical characteristics. The major difference between building a cage for a cabochon and building one for a marble is that you need more binding wraps to hold a cabochon in place. The placement of these binding wraps is not as arbitrary as may initially seem. You've really got to be sure that the stone has no place to go once you're finished. Nothing would be more embarrassing than showing off your beautifully wrapped cabochon, only to have it slip out the side of your cage the first time someone picks it up!

For a relatively flat, rectangular stone like the ones shown (okay, the cabochons wrapped here are actually oval, but for the purpose of placing binding wraps you should think of them as rectangular: two long sides, two short sides), you want to use at least four binding wraps, one at each side. The top will have the exact same kind of collar that we built for the marble pendant. The bottom and two sides will have the same binding wraps that we placed at the bottom of the marble pendant.

For a cabochon cage you'll need

20 gauge (0.8mm) half-hard round wire

round nose pliers

chain nose pliers

flush cutters

crimp forming pliers

flat nose pliers

a cabochon (approximately 30mm × 40mm works well, and it's a relatively readily available size)

a rubber band, (one of those thick ones that newspaper carriers or postal workers use)

a pen (one that will leave marks on the wire, such as a fine point Sharpie™)

1 Cut five pieces of wire as follows: two 12" pieces and three 3" pieces. Pull them all straight.

Actually, the lengths of the wire pieces you will be using to build the bars and collar of the cage will vary depending on the size of the stone or cabochon you want to wrap. Generally, for a basically rectangular stone less than 1" thick, you can use a piece of wire that is 4 times the height plus 5". This will give you enough wire to completely circumnavigate the stone, build a collar, and leave a little wire to hold onto while you are pulling that last wire wrap around the collar. (I've thrown in an extra inch in the directions here to give you just a little more breathing room the first time around.)

2 Place your first binding wrap (as shown in Steps 4 through 7 of the marble cage on pages 85–86) about 3" from one end.

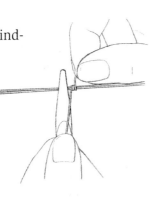

3 On your worktable, hold the binding wrap against the bottom of your cabochon with the thumb of your non-dominant hand.

4 Pull both sets of wires up (one at a time) and around onto the top of the cabochon, holding them onto the sides with the index and middle fingers of your non-dominant hand. Make sure that the wire is pulled tightly onto the entire outer diameter of the cabochon.

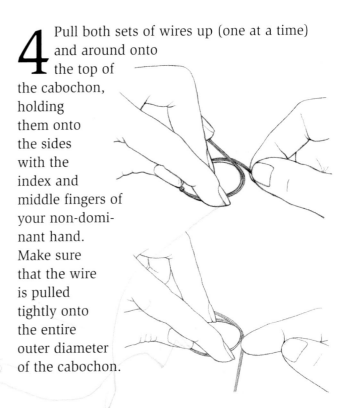

5 Pick the cage up off the cabochon. Don't worry—the wire will more or less remember the shape. Push the cage back into the shape of the cabochon, being careful not to make it smaller.

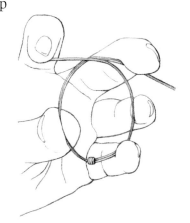

7 Using the pen marks as guides, pull both sets of wires up and away from the big oval loop so that the bends are just about 90° angles.

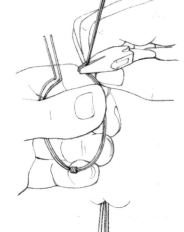

6 Draw a line across all four pieces of wire at the top, directly opposite the bottom wrap. I can't stress enough how important it is that these guide marks be *exactly* the same distance from the bottom wrap.

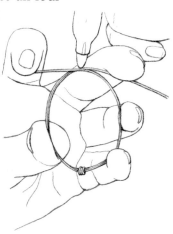

All four wires should line up flush when you push both sets of wire closed.

Now you are ready to place the other two binding wraps on the cage. These will be approximately halfway between the bottom wrap and the collar. It is also very important to space these wraps exactly the same distance from the bottom wrap.

8 Hold one side of the cage in chain nose pliers at the halfway point between the bottom wrap and the bend that will become part of the collar. The cage should be oriented in your pliers so that you are looking down at the inside. This way you'll be able to tweak the tail ends of the binding wraps down onto the inside of your cage, and they won't be visible when you're finished.

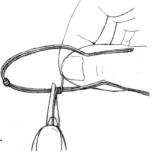

9 Place three nice tight wraps on this side of your cage. Snip the ends but don't tweak them down.

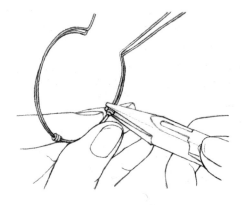

10 Repeat Steps 8 and 9 on the other side of the cage. Make sure that both binding wraps on the side are the same distance away from the bottom wrap. Since the ends have not yet been tweaked down, you should be able to move the binding wraps easily. Once they are equidistant, tweak them down as in Step 7 of the marble wraps.

11 You should have two short and two long wires sticking out from the top of the cage. Snip the two short ones down to ¼" and bend one of the longer pieces to a nice sharp 90° angle. The bend has to be exactly ¼" away from the loop, flush with the two smaller ends you've just snipped.

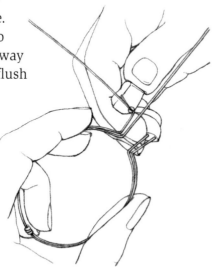

12 Bend the other long piece of wire away from the first to not quite a 90° angle.

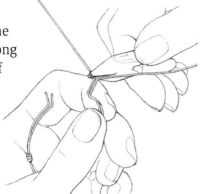

13 Make a loop with the first piece of wire you bent to 90°. Holding the loop with the long piece of wire pointing toward you, and your palm out, grasp the wire with round nose pliers about ¼" away from the bend and complete the loop.

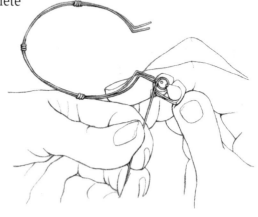

14 Using the outside station of crimp forming pliers, gather all four pieces of wire that bend up off the loop and hold the pliers closed. The pliers should be placed right up against the shoulder of the cage. Wrap a rubber band three or four times around the handles of the pliers to keep them held closed. You can now work with both hands while the crimping pliers hold everything together.

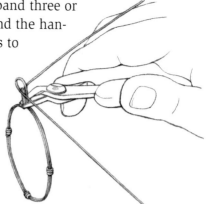

15 Holding the chain nose pliers in your non-dominant hand and sticking straight out in front of you, grasp the loop you've made in the top of the collar.

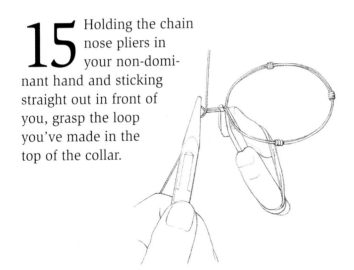

the collar. *Note:* These wraps should start underneath the last long piece that you bent to not quite 90°.

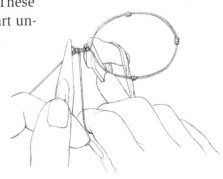

16 Pull the wire from the loop around *all four* pieces of wire that are being held together by the crimping pliers. Start wrapping slowly, forming nice, even, perpendicular, and most importantly tight wraps all the way up to the crimping pliers.

Pull the wraps most of the way around, until the crimping pliers are in the way, then let go, grasp the wire again from underneath, and repeat. You should end up with at least three or four tight wraps on

17 Remove the rubber band from the crimping pliers and pull the pliers off the collar. You can now continue pulling nice tight wraps all the way down to the shoulder of the cage. Once you've finished wrapping, snip the end down and tweak it flat onto the collar.

18 Snip the last piece of wire that bends out from the top of the collar down to about 1½". Make a flat scroll (see pages 30–31) perpendicular to the collar.

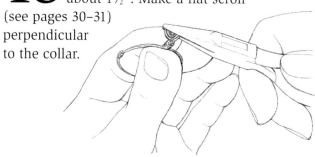

19 Using chain nose pliers, very slightly spread open the four sections of wire that are between the binding wraps.

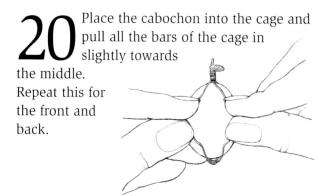

20 Place the cabochon into the cage and pull all the bars of the cage in slightly towards the middle. Repeat this for the front and back.

Now that the cabochon is more or less in place, you will need to make small bends (very much like the zigzags we made in the marble wraps) to take up the slack and hold the stone tightly. Make these bends with flat nose pliers.

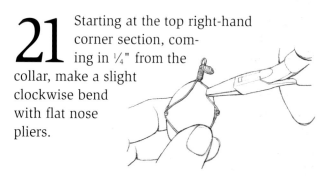

21 Starting at the top right-hand corner section, coming in ¼" from the collar, make a slight clockwise bend with flat nose pliers.

22 Moving down about ¼" from that bend, make a slight counter-clockwise bend.

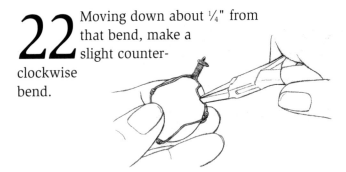

These two bends effectively pull the wire in toward the center of the cabochon and then back out again towards the binding wrap. Repeat these clockwise/counterclockwise bends around all four sections in front and then again in back. The end result should look like this.

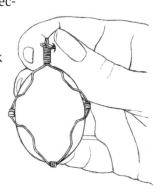

23 Finally, pull the loop perpendicular to the front of the cabochon and pull the flat scroll down onto the front of the collar.

Chapter 9

GALLERY OF CONTEMPORARY WIREWORK

The work on the following pages comes from twelve contemporary wire artists, including myself. I hope these pieces inspire you to use your newfound skills and create your own original works of art, whether they are jewelry, sculptures, or other objects.

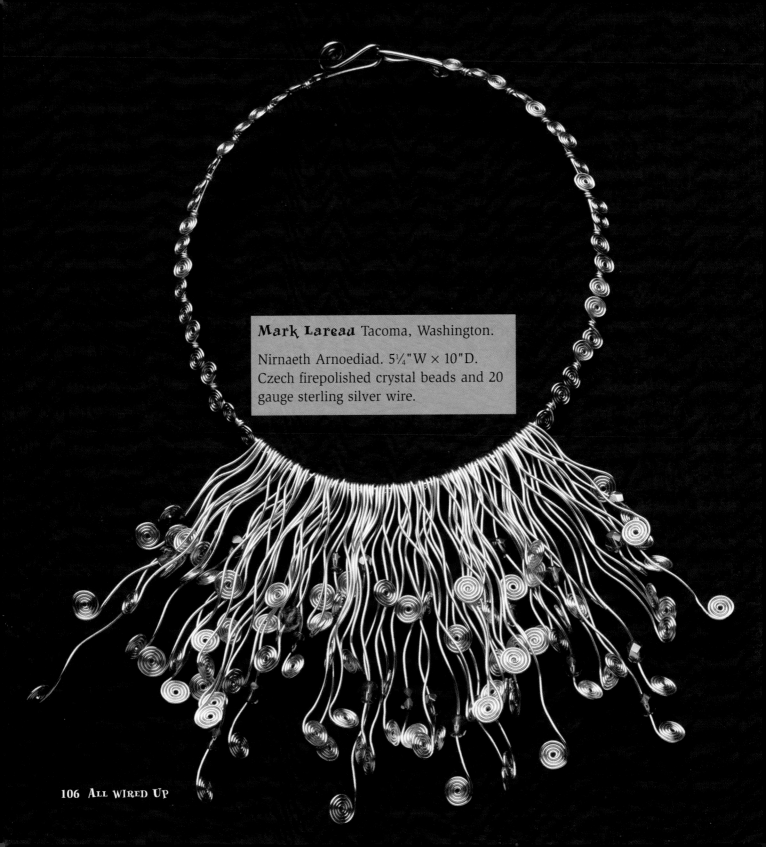

Mark Lareau Tacoma, Washington.

Nirnaeth Arnoediad. 5¼"W × 10"D.
Czech firepolished crystal beads and 20
gauge sterling silver wire.